John Paul Jones, America's Sailor

A Naval Institute Book for Young Readers

JOHN PAUL JONES
America's Sailor

Clara Ann Simmons

Naval Institute Press
Annapolis, Maryland

Library of Congress Cataloging-in-Publication Data
Simmons, Clara Ann, 1923–
    John Paul Jones, America's sailor / Clara Ann Simmons.
      p. cm. — (A Naval Institute book for young readers)
    Includes index.
    Summary: Describes the life of the Revolutionary War hero, from his birth to his burial at the United States Naval Academy.
    ISBN 1-55750-833-X (alk. paper)
    1. Jones, John Paul, 1747–1792—Juvenile literature. 2. Sailors—United States—Biography—Juvenile literature. 3. United States. Navy—Biography—Juvenile literature. 4. United States—History—Revolution, 1775–1783—Naval operations—Juvenile literature. [1. Jones, John Paul, 1747–1792. 2. Admirals. 3. United States. Navy—Biography. 4. United States—History—Revolution. 1775–1783—Biography.]
I. Title. II. Series.
E207.J7S716 1996
973.3'5'092—dc2O
[B]   96-30512

Printed in the United States of America on acid-free paper ∞

04 03 02 01 00 99 98 97   9 8 7 6 5 4 3 2
First printing

For Ellen and Kenneth

Contents

John Paul Jones, America's Sailor

1

John Paul, Young Seaman

When America's sailor was a boy his name was John Paul. When he grew up he changed it to John Paul Jones, but he never changed what he wanted to be: a sailor who found fame and glory.

From his earliest days by the Solway Firth where he was born on July 6, 1747, he watched all manner of ships sailing up and down that bay and out to sea. The Solway Firth is a big bay dividing Scotland from England, and John Paul lived right along it in a white cottage on an estate called Arbigland. His father was the head gardener on the estate, which was near the town of Kirkcudbright. John Paul lived there with his parents, his three sisters—Elizabeth, Janet, and Mary Ann—and his brother William, who left home when John Paul was very young. Life was happy in his warm, cozy home; the family had plenty of food from the gardens and fish from the clean and sparkling bay and rivers.

People remembered that whenever he and his playmates sailed their toy boats along the shore, John Paul was always the captain of the ships. He would stand on the highest ground and give orders

When America's sailor was a boy, he lived in this cottage
on the Solway Firth in Scotland.

to his squadron. The boys rowed about in boats and knew how to handle small sailboats because in those days, one of the most important ways to travel was by water.

Young John Paul would talk to the fishermen and learn about the best places to catch salmon. They might also have told him exciting tales of the smugglers on the nearby Isle of Man, in the Irish Sea. He would watch the many merchant ships sailing toward the nearby town of Dumfries, on the River Nith. They brought tar and tobacco from Virginia in the American colonies, wine from Portugal, and timber from the Baltic Sea regions, as well as goods from other lands. John Paul would talk to the sailors about faraway places and dreamed of visiting them. He already knew about Virginia because William had gone there to live. William was a tailor in Fredericksburg, a busy port on the Rappahannock River.

When John Paul was old enough, he went to the parish school a mile from his home. There he studied reading, writing, arithmetic, Latin, and French. He liked to learn new things because he wanted to get ahead and see the world. One of the studies he liked best was navigation. It is not surprising, then, that when he turned thirteen—the time to begin earning his own living—he chose to go to sea. His parents apprenticed him to James Younger, a merchant shipper in Whitehaven, England, a fishing port across the bay from Kirkcudbright. As a young boy, John Paul had probably been there several times with his father. He was bound to serve Mr. Younger as an apprentice seaman for seven years and soon went aboard the *Friendship* under Captain Robert Benson.

Life at sea in the eighteenth century was not easy. The wooden ships were powered by sail. A brig like the *Friendship* would have two masts, larger ships would have three. Each mast supported many sails of different sizes. Each sail was controlled by a great many ropes called the running rigging. A sailor had to know which sail each rope went to, and he had to be able to handle the rigging during fierce storms, when waves washed over the ship or when it was so cold the sea spray froze on the ropes.

At the stern of the larger ships the captain had a cabin and his own dining room where he entertained guests. The officers had their quarters and dining room in the rear of the brig too. But the crew lived in the bow of the ship in very crowded conditions. They slept in hammocks slung side by side. They had to roll them up and stash them away each morning. They ate on long tables that were hung between the mounted guns (even merchant ships had to have guns on board with which to fight pirates). The crew hoisted up the tables when they were not being used.

Their food was cooked in the galley amidships. That meant the ship had to have wood on board for cook fires and a smokestack sticking up through the deck. Most of the time the crew ate salt pork, peas, a biscuit called hardtack, and beans. If they were lucky they caught fresh fish or got fresh fruit and vegetables when the ship anchored in a port. They had to carry enough water in wooden casks to last them for months while they crossed the oceans. Sometimes there was a cow on board so that there would be fresh milk for anyone who got sick.

The sailors had to scrape and scrub the decks every day and keep everything shipshape. Fearsome things happened to them if they did not do their work. The boatswain in charge of the crew kept a knotted rope in his hand. If the sailors did not work fast enough, he lashed them with the rope. The worst offenders were keelhauled. This meant the man's hands and feet were tied together. Then he was thrown overboard and pulled under the ship (below the keel) from one side to the other. Keelhauled sailors almost drowned.

But there were also good things about life at sea. The sailors knew they would have a place to sleep and food to eat and they would be paid for their work at the end of the voyage. Often, at home on land, work was hard to find. Once the sailors learned their daily chores, they discovered the work was not too hard. In the daytime they would gather around the scuttlebutt, a big cask full of water, and gossip while they got a drink. In the evenings the sailors

A captain's cabin had space enough for a private dining area where
he could entertain guests. John Paul would someday
have a place like this on board his warships.

The sailors relaxed in their quarters after their chores were done.

entertained each other with stories. Someone might play a fiddle. There would be dancing, singing, or wrestling.

No doubt young John Paul looked forward to his first trip on the *Friendship*. The ship was bound for the West Indies with a load of English goods. This first trip turned out to be a good lesson in what could happen to a small, wooden ship as it crossed the Atlantic Ocean. When the *Friendship* was about halfway across, the winds died. The ship was becalmed for almost two weeks. It was hard for the boatswain to keep the sailors busy. Their food and water probably had to be rationed so that it would last. Later in the trip they ran into rough seas and a storm full of hail, sleet, and snow. This time the sailors had a lot to do to keep the vessel afloat.

At last they reached Barbados in the Caribbean Sea. Here the captain sold his cargo of English goods and bought rum and sugar. He sailed north to the Chesapeake Bay, then on up the Rappahannock River to the port of Fredericksburg. There he sold the rum and sugar and bought tobacco, pig iron, and barrel staves to carry back to Whitehaven to sell. Usually the *Friendship* made one trip a year from Whitehaven to Barbados to Fredericksburg and home again.

When the ship got to Virginia the crew knew they would stay there a while to unload the goods and to take on new supplies. They might also have to scrape the barnacles off the bottom of the ship and repair any damage to the hull and masts caused by storms. The sailors stayed on the ship, but John Paul was lucky; he got to stay in town in his brother's comfortable home and to help William in his tailor shop. John Paul also spent time reading and studying geography, mathematics, French, and navigation. He said he burned the midnight oil studying because he had made up his mind to be a success. He learned to express himself very well by writing.

The one thing he did not learn to do was control his temper. John Paul had a violent temper that got him into deep trouble more than once in his life. It even changed his way of living later on.

As the town tailor, William Paul knew many of the gentry, including George Washington's sister Betty and her husband, Fielding

John Paul helped his brother, William, in his tailor shop when he came to Fredericksburg. Some people think it was in this corner house on Caroline Street.

Lewis. This couple were important shippers and merchants and probably sold provisions and tobacco to the *Friendship*'s captain. John Paul saw the refined way these people lived. Fielding and Betty Lewis's beautiful brick home, Kenmore, was full of fine silver, crystal, books, and furniture from England. He realized that gentlemen dressed well and spoke proper English. He determined to get rid of his Scots brogue.

When he visited Fredericksburg, young John Paul often saw
this beautiful brick home, called Kenmore, owned by
Betty and Fielding Lewis.

John Paul was released from his apprenticeship after just a few
years because Mr. Younger's business failed. That meant he had to
find another way to earn his living at sea.

2

Merchant Seaman

When John Paul was seventeen years old he was about 5'5" tall and had freckles and hazel-colored eyes. He wore his sandy-brown hair pulled back in a ponytail. He spoke softly and politely when in company and was always neatly dressed.

He had sailed over much of the world. Now he wanted to make money and get to know important people. In one of his letters, he spoke of wanting to find a place of contentment. Perhaps he would make enough money to buy a farm and settle down on land. One way to get rich quickly in the 1760s was to be a slave trader. There was a saying "As wealthy as a West Indian." A West Indian was another name for a slave trader.

The trader would pick up the slaves in West Africa and sail them to the West Indies. They were packed in the ships like sardines in a tin and treated like animals. They lay side by side in the hold, ate bad food, and had no way to keep clean. (But a trader did want the slaves on his ship to stay healthy so he could sell them all.) Once the ships got to the West Indies, the slaves were sold and the trader

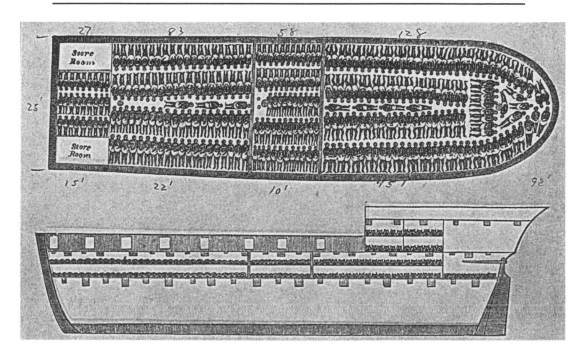

These drawings show how crowded the slave ships were in what
John Paul called an "abominable trade."

bought rum and sugar. He sold this in the American colonies and bought tobacco to sail back to England.

John Paul called it an "abominable trade," and after two years he quit to sail on other ships. By now he knew a ship inside and out, from stern to bow. He could bring a ship safely through all kinds of weather and navigate all sorts of bays, rivers, and oceans. He was hired to command the *John,* a merchant ship that sailed from Whitehaven to Tobago in the Caribbean Sea. As captain, he kept complete control of the ship and crew. His rules were strict, and he punished men who did not obey them.

One of the men he punished was Mungo Maxwell, the ship's carpenter. Maxwell came from John Paul's hometown. On their second trip Maxwell did something that annoyed the captain. John Paul lost his fiery temper and had Maxwell tied up and lashed. He accused Maxwell of not doing his work well and of disobeying orders. But Maxwell went to the naval court on Tobago and filed a complaint against Captain Paul. The judge knew that sailors were often lashed for not obeying orders. He decreed that Maxwell's beating did not seem to have been too harsh.

Maxwell left the merchant ship *John* and shipped for home on another vessel. He died on the way. When news of this reached his parents in Kirkcudbright, they went to court and charged the captain with murder. Captain Paul arrived in Scotland in November 1770 and found there was a warrant out for his arrest. He was immediately locked up in the local jail. This was serious trouble.

But John Paul got himself released on bail and spent the next two years working to regain his good name. He sailed back to the West Indies and got a letter from the lieutenant governor who declared him innocent of causing Maxwell's death. John Paul then traveled to London and secured a letter from the captain of the vessel Maxwell had sailed toward home on. The captain stated that Maxwell died of low spirits and a fever. John Paul's case was finally dismissed and he was free to sail again.

During this time John Paul joined a Masonic lodge in Kirkcud-bright. The Freemasons are a club of men bound together by a secret oath and a pledge to help one another. Belonging to the Masons was a good way for him to meet important citizens. There had been a lodge at Fredericksburg, Virginia, since 1752. Perhaps while he lived there with his brother he first learned about Freemasonry. As a Mason John Paul could go to any lodge to meet and discuss events with its members. Even in Kirkcudbright in 1770 he might have begun to hear that the American colonies were getting angry at King George III.

In 1772 John Paul and a partner bought the merchant ship *Betsy*. They were clever traders and soon became rich. John Paul bought land in the American colonies and other countries and invested his money in stocks. Everything was going just right for him until the *Betsy's* trip to Tobago in 1773, when an event happened that was to change his life forever. He called it "the greatest misfortune of my life."

The *Betsy* had sailed from England, and when she got to Tobago the crew rebelled because they had not been paid. Sailors in those days did not get paid on a regular basis. They got their money all at once after the ship's master had sold his cargo. The *Betsy's* crew complained that they had not been paid for fourteen months. Captain John Paul promised he would pay them when they got back to England, but that did not calm them. He then passed out new clothing among them, but this did not quiet them.

The crew decided to desert the ship. Just before they climbed into the ship's boat, the ringleader grabbed a bludgeon and went for the captain. John Paul had gone to his cabin to get his sword. His temper flared; he would not have such disobedience on board his ship. The ringleader came at him with the huge club. The captain plunged his sword into the man, instantly killing him. Once again John Paul found himself called a murderer.

The naval court was not sitting on Tobago at that time. John Paul knew he would have to wait on the island until the court returned and

John Paul killed a rebellious crewman on board the *Betsy* and called that terrible event "the greatest misfortune" of his life.

could try his case. His friends were afraid that he would be attacked by angry seamen if he stayed. They persuaded him to flee and stay away until the court returned. They advised him to travel incognito to North America. He took only fifty pounds of British currency and fled.

Little is known about him for almost two years. Even afterward, in writing to Benjamin Franklin about this part of his life, he never told what happened. He said only that strangers helped him. Some people guessed that he sailed the North Atlantic coast as a privateer; others that he spent the time on a plantation in North Carolina. Whatever he did, we can safely guess that he got to know rich planters, important statesmen, and politicians.

A portrait of North Carolina Congressman
Joseph Hewes by artist C. W. Peale. Hewes used
his influence to get John Paul Jones a commission
in the Continental Navy.

John Paul also knew that the colonists were getting angrier and
angrier about the taxes King George III was putting on goods
shipped to them. In 1773 the people of Boston threw a shipload of
tea overboard because they did not want to pay the hated British
import tax. In 1774 men from each of the thirteen colonies met in
Philadelphia to decide to break away from England. They were
called the First Continental Congress. In April 1775 British soldiers
fired on the citizens of Concord, Massachusetts, and the Revolutionary War began.

In the summer of 1775, John Paul Jones, Esquire, a well-dressed young man with good manners, appeared in Philadelphia. This was the same John Paul who had fled Tobago two years before, but now, at twenty-eight, he was bold, brash, and had added Jones to his name. He wanted to go to sea again, this time to fight for liberty. He became a friend of Joseph Hewes, a member of Congress from North Carolina. Mr. Hewes used his influence to get his seafaring friend just the job he wanted.

On December 7, 1775, John Paul Jones, Esquire, was commissioned a first lieutenant in the Continental Navy. And what a struggling navy it was.

3

John Paul Jones, Young Captain

When the British redcoats fired on the American colonists at Lexington and Concord there was no Continental Navy. For that matter, there was not even an army! But an army was quickly assembled, and George Washington of Virginia was made its commander in chief. He believed the colonies needed a navy to defend the cities along the Atlantic Coast. Washington realized that the British had one of the best navies in the world. He knew they would use it to ship men, guns, and supplies to their fighting men in America. A Continental Navy could capture these ships and take the needed supplies for the colonists' own army.

Some men agreed that a country with a long coastline needed a navy; some said it was a crazy idea. While the members of Congress argued about this, Washington used some of the new government's money to buy the schooner *Hannah*. He had her armed as the first ship in service. The *Hannah* went to sea off the coast of Massachusetts early in September 1775 and captured his majesty's ship (HMS) *Unity*, which was full of supplies the Continental Army could use.

HOPKINS COMMANDANT EN CHEF
la Flote Américaine

The old sea captain Esek Hopkins was appointed
commander of the new Continental Navy.

Some of the southern colonies decided to create their own navies instead of waiting for Congress to act. They wanted to have their cities protected while they were waiting for Congress to vote for a navy. Finally, after much arguing, Congress appointed seven men to a Naval Committee in the fall of 1775.

Starting a navy was not an easy thing to do. It took as long as a year to build just one of the wooden warships and fit it out with sails, ropes, guns, and supplies. The new government did not have much money to spend on these men-of-war. It decided to give letters of marque to more than a thousand merchant ships. These ships were called privateers because they were owned by private citizens. A letter of marque meant the ships' captains had the government's permission to attack and capture enemy vessels and take the cargo as a prize and the crew as prisoners. The privateers then sold the cargo, and all of the money went to the owners and crew. This was a good way to capture British ships and help win the war. But the sailors on privateers enjoyed their prize money so much they did not want to join the new navy, which could pay them very little.

Since they did not have the time or the money to build new ships, the Naval Committee decided to buy merchant ships and convert them into warships. They bought four such ships and renamed them the *Alfred, Columbus, Andrew Doria,* and *Cabot.* Esek Hopkins, an old sea captain from Providence, Rhode Island, was appointed to command this fleet. When he got to Philadelphia he gave Lieutenant John Paul Jones charge of the *Alfred* until her captain would arrive from New England.

The new fleet had not received its orders from the Naval Committee. December 1775 in Philadelphia was very cold, and the Delaware River so frozen, that the fleet could not sail. John Paul Jones knew he had to keep his crew busy to keep them from deserting. He did this by having them practice gun drills over and over again so the gunners would be well trained for battle.

It took about seven men to man each cannon. They had to open the wooden gun ports, then pull the muzzle through the port using

John Paul Jones and a gun crew on the *Bonhomme Richard.*
The crew he drilled on the *Alfred* in the winter of 1775
might have looked like this.

John Paul Jones loved to fly big flags like this one, with its eight-pointed stars and red, white, and blue stripes.

ropes. Many tools with names like rammer, powder horn, spike, and quoin had to be at hand. Bags full of black powder had to be ready, along with plenty of cannonballs or shot. The sailors had to follow command without a mistake. "Take out your tompions" meant remove the stoppers in the muzzles. "Shot your guns" meant ram in the cannonball. There were many steps until the word "Fire" was shouted. Lieutenant Jones was proud of his crew; they performed each gun drill quickly, without any mistakes. But he never praised them. As a result, he was a lonely man.

Another act of which he was very proud was that he ran up the country's new flag on the *Alfred*. As he later wrote in one of his many letters, "I hoisted with my own hands, the Flag of Freedom for the first time it was displayed. . . ." This was the new Grand Union Flag made by Margaret Manny of Philadelphia. It had thirteen red and white stripes and the crosses of St. George and St. Andrew. John

The *Alfred* flies the new country's Grand Union Flag on her stern.
John Paul Jones hoisted the new flag of freedom—
the first time it was ever displayed.

Paul Jones liked to use large flags on whatever ship he commanded. He especially liked ones with red, white, and blue stripes and stars with at least eight points.

The Naval Committee now issued orders to Commodore Hopkins. He was to sail his fleet to the Chesapeake Bay and capture the British ships commanded by Lord Dunmore. But the fleet's commander did not like that idea. And since his orders stated he could follow a course of his best judgment, he took his fleet to the Bahamas where there was a large supply of ammunition at the fort at Nassau. His fleet captured the fort and started to sail back north.

By April 4, 1776, the *Alfred* and her crew had rendezvoused at Block Island with the fleet and taken the enemy brig *Bolton* and schooner *Hawk*. Two days later, the fleet met and engaged HMS *Glasgow* for three hours. It should have been an easy battle, four ships against one. But the *Alfred* got broadside to the wind and was raked with gunfire. A shot carried away her wheel block and the lines to the tiller. The ship could not be steered. While this was going on, Jones was in charge of the lower gun deck, giving orders to the men he had trained so well. Other members of the crew were finally able to repair the tiller, and Commodore Hopkins ordered the *Alfred* to return to port.

Officers and crew who had done the fighting criticized the commodore for leaving the fight. John Paul Jones did not like criticism of any kind. He often wrote long letters defending his actions. He would blame everybody else if things went wrong. If things went well, he would heap praise on his own actions. So he wrote to his old friend Joseph Hewes explaining that he had been in the lower gun deck during the fight. The *Alfred's* poor showing was not his fault; his gun crews had fired as ordered. But Congress praised Commodore Hopkins for getting his fleet, and the prizes they had captured, safely to New London, Connecticut.

On May 10, 1776, Commodore Hopkins gave Lieutenant Jones command of the sloop *Providence* and the temporary rank of captain. John Paul Jones loved the *Providence;* she was sleek and fast with her one large mast. He liked to sail at full speed, which means with all the sails set. Then, running with the wind, he would lead his enemy on a merry chase and play tricks on him. He needed a fast ship to do this.

The crew of about seventy-five officers and men was much to his liking, but the feeling was not mutual. Sailors were never devoted to John Paul Jones. He was very strict, he felt he was always right, and he did not discuss his plans with his officers or men. He kept aloof from the crew and never gave them cause to love him. But they also knew he could sail rings around any other captain. They could be certain his ship would be scrubbed clean and full of the best provisions he could find.

Now Jones and his crew were ready to have some good times cruising the western Atlantic in the *Providence*. First, they did some conveying between New England and New York, taking soldiers back to their camps. This was easy work. Then, on August 6, 1776, the Marine Committee (as the Naval Committee was called by that time) gave the lieutenant orders to cruise around for three months and "Seize, take, Sink, Burn or destroy" the enemy's ships. He was to assist any American ships that were in trouble. If he found out any enemy secrets, he was to put into port right away and send a letter to the committee. John Paul Jones could scarcely wait to get started. He would sail all over the Atlantic Ocean, from Bermuda to Newfoundland.

Two days later—August 8, 1776—the Marine Committee made him a naval captain. John Paul Jones was not happy, though. He argued loudly that his commission should have been dated May tenth, the date when he was first made temporary captain. This would have given him seniority over other captains, but the date was not changed.

The *Providence* began cruising and almost immediately captured a British whaler. Captain Jones put a prize crew on her and sent her back to Philadelphia. One of the problems with the prize ships was that good crew members had to be put on them to take them into

John Paul Jones loved the sleek, fast sloop *Providence*.
Here he is, hailing the flagship *Alfred*.

friendly ports where the cargo could be sold. If a lot of prize ships were taken, many of the crew would have to leave the ship. Sometimes a prize ship had to be sunk because there were not enough men to sail it.

After about a month of roaming the Atlantic Ocean, the captain decided to sail into a port in Nova Scotia to restock food and water. The ship also hove to so the crew could catch some fresh fish to eat. Soon after, they sighted a British frigate bearing down on them. John Paul Jones quickly hoisted sail on his fast sloop. In the chase that followed he tempted the frigate to fire even though the British were too far away to do any damage. When the enemy sent his last broadside toward the *Providence,* the feisty captain made fun of him by answering with a single musket shot.

When the cruise was over, John Paul Jones was again made captain of the *Alfred* and went to Newfoundland to destroy fishing boats that provided food for the British army. The *Alfred* captured a most important prize ship, HMS *Mellish,* which was full of warm winter uniforms. The British said the capture was "trifling," but John Paul Jones knew better. The badly needed supplies were sent to Washington's army before the Battle of Trenton.

When the *Alfred* got to port, Captain Jones paid the crew their share of the prize money out of his own pocket. None of them knew he did this, and it was not until after the end of the war that Congress paid him back.

Sailing back toward Boston, John Paul Jones and the *Alfred* met HMS *Milford.* He decided to have some fun. He hoisted a light to the top of his ship's mainmast and told his officers sailing the prize ships to go full speed ahead. The clever captain tacked, and the *Milford* followed the *Alfred*'s light and zigzag course instead of going after the prizes.

In October 1776, Congress published a new list of twenty-four naval captains. John Paul Jones was number eighteen. This did not please him one bit. He knew he was far superior to many others on

Many artists painted portraits of the dashing
naval officer. This engraving was done by
Jean Michel Moreau le Jeune of Paris.

the list. He said they could not read and did not even know how to
command a merchant vessel. He wrote letters to a lot of people saying the list was not fair.

The list was not changed, but on June 14, 1777, Congress
appointed Captain John Paul Jones to command the new frigate
Ranger. That was also the day the Stars and Stripes was adopted as
the country's new flag. It was a good beginning for the flag and for
the captain.

4

The *Ranger* Raids

Captain Jones went to Portsmouth, New Hampshire, where the *Ranger* and many other ships had been built. The town had a good protected harbor, and it was surrounded by tall pine trees that were sawed into masts and spars.

The captain's new ship was being fitted out. John Paul Jones always loved to take charge of this part of shipbuilding, but he was furious at what he saw. He complained to Colonel John Langdon, who built the fast sloop of war, that the sails were made of cheap hessian instead of good sturdy canvas. He said the masts were too long and heavy and that the spars should be smaller. He griped that the ship was too light for the number of guns on board and it carried fewer than thirty gallons of rum. That was not enough to make the crew happy. There were not even any boatswain's whistles.

As he usually did, John Paul Jones wrote letters to important men listing all the things he thought were wrong in the *Ranger*. In those letters he said that instead of helping him, the captain, fit out the ship, Colonel Langdon had the nerve to think he could do it him-

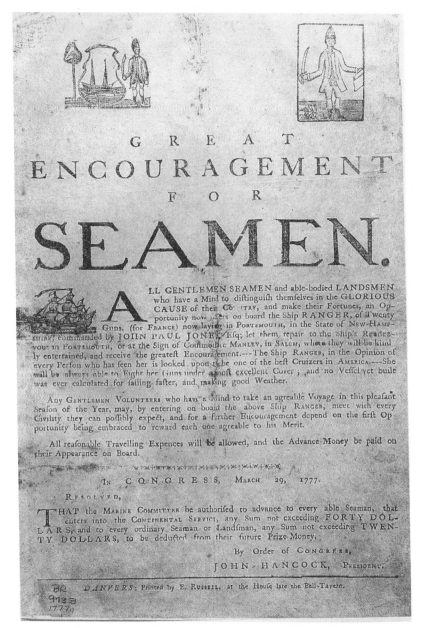

This printed "broadside" was used to recruit seamen for the new ship "RANGER, of Twenty Guns (for France)." These announcements were probably posted in taverns and public buildings.

self. John Paul Jones used his own money to buy silver boatswain's whistles and live chickens to take on board the ship. He likewise used his own money to buy a supply of new clothes, or "slops" as they called them, for the crew.

Besides fussing and fuming about getting the *Ranger* fitted out just as he wanted, Captain Jones had to worry about getting the crew. It was not easy to find men who wanted to be navy sailors because they could make more money on privateers.

The young captain went through the town accompanied by two men. One man beat a drum and the other one carried a flag to attract attention. John Paul Jones, under authority of Congress, promised that any man who signed on would get an advance of money and a share of any prizes the *Ranger* and her crew seized.

By November 1, 1777, a crew of 150 men, the supplies, and the *Ranger* were finally ready. They set sail for France with a special message for Benjamin Franklin. The message was that on October 17, British General John Burgoyne had surrendered his whole army to America's General Horatio Gates at Saratoga. This was an important battle for America to win, as it kept the British from dividing New York. Such news would make Benjamin Franklin happy. He, Silas Deane, and Arthur Lee had been sent by Congress to ask France to help the colonies in their fight against England. One of the ways France could help was by allowing American ships of war to use busy French ports along the Bay of Biscay.

After a fast trip, the *Ranger* arrived at one of those ports, Paimboeuf, on December second. Before he sailed from Portsmouth, John Paul Jones had been told that he would get command of a frigate, the *L'Indien,* which was being built in Holland. One of the first things he wanted to do, of course, was see about this new ship. To keep the crew happy while he was away, Captain Jones ordered Lieutenant Thomas Simpson to buy fresh meat, greens, and brandy for his men. The captain also gave orders to have the sloop careened and greaved, that is, to heel the ship over and scrape the bottom. He arranged for new sails to be made; the old ones were used to make new hammocks for the men.

John Paul Jones left for Paris on his two matters of business. He met Benjamin Franklin at Passy, right outside Paris. Franklin became the captain's patron, and they wrote many letters to each other thereafter. Benjamin Franklin always supported his young friend and often gave him advice. One of the best pieces of advice was that John Paul Jones should learn to praise his officers and crew. He never did, though, and he never rewarded bravery.

It wasn't long before Captain Jones learned that the Dutch had decided to sell the *L'Indien* to the French government instead of to America. He was greatly disappointed because this meant he would have to continue commanding the *Ranger.*

John Paul Jones decided to spend some time sailing around the Bay of Biscay so his crew could become familiar with the ports. They might have to take quick refuge in any one of them if the British pursued them. At Quiberon Bay the *Ranger* met a French squadron under the command of Admiral La Motte Piquet. Here was Captain Jones's chance to be recognized as an equal. He sent a brash note to Piquet calling for a thirteen-gun salute. Piquet wrote back that Jones could salute him with thirteen, but he would return only a nine-gun salute. Captain Jones was angry, but there was not much he could do except fire a thirteen-gun salute and receive the nine-gun one in return. Still, he could brag that it was the first time the Stars and Stripes had been saluted at sea.

On April 10, 1778, he and the *Ranger* set off on a cruise that was to make them famous. They sailed up the Irish Sea toward the Scottish captain's hometown on the Solway Firth. John Paul Jones knew these waters very well and didn't have to worry about unknown shoals or rocks. On the way he and his crew took two prize ships and had a skirmish with one of the enemy's cutters.

Captain Jones made a bold plan to attack Whitehaven, the port from which he sailed when he was thirteen. Nobody had yet attacked British ports although the British had attacked and burned

John Paul Jones wrote many letters. This one was sent from the *Ranger* on February 13, 1778, requesting that Admiral La Motte Piquet exchange a salute "gun for gun."

Aboard the *Ranger,* Captain Jones exchanges salutes in
Quiberon Bay with the French admiral.

American towns. Now John Paul Jones would do the same to them.

Whitehaven's harbor was divided into two parts by a stone pier. Since there was no wind of any kind to drive the *Ranger,* the captain decided to attack with the two ship's boats. The crew of one would go to the south harbor, the other to the north. They were to spike the harbor guns and set fire to all the vessels in port. Around midnight on April 22, 1778, forty officers and men set out in the two boats. It took them three hours to row to Whitehaven. Once they got there, things did not go according to the captain's plan.

The crew that was to attack the north harbor headed for the nearest pub. What they really wanted to do was attack merchant ships, capture them, and get a lot of prize money. They were not at all for burning some fishing boats. Besides, their captain had not even discussed his plans with his officers or crew. So they settled down in the pub and helped themselves to rum and ale.

One of the sailors felt it was not fair for Captain Jones to attack his old neighbors. He ran from house to house, knocking on the doors and yelling that the Americans were coming. It is a good thing Captain Jones did not know about this. He and his crew were busy scaling the wall of the south harbor. When they got over the top, they began to spike the guns. They could not set fire to the ships right away, though, because they had lost their light and tinder. One of them had to go to a nearby house to ask for a light.

By this time many Whitehaven citizens had been roused from their homes and had run down to defend their harbor. Captain Jones and his crew had just enough time to tip a barrel of tar over a collier, light it, and start a mighty fire. Then the raiders fled to their boat, and both crews rowed back to the *Ranger.* All the while the British townspeople were on the dock firing away with muskets. John Paul Jones was disappointed in the crew's actions during the raid, but he did not punish the seamen who went to the pub or the one who alerted the citizens. He simply determined to continue harassing the towns along the west coast of England.

After the raid on Whitehaven, the frightened British
called John Paul Jones a "pirate."

The frightened people of Whitehaven did not know if this raid was just the start of more to come. They did not know if other parts of the country would also be raided. All up and down the coastline the citizens got out their swords and muskets and anything else they thought they could use to defend themselves.

The newspapers wrote chilling accounts of the daring attack. Citizens demanded to know why the Royal Navy was not defending their seas. They were amazed to find out that the captain of this attack was once their neighbor, John Paul. Now they called John Paul Jones a pirate.

Captain Jones decided on yet another kind of raid. He would attack the estate of a rich person, seize that person, and hold him hostage. Then he would tell the British that he would set the captive free if they would free American sailors in their prisons. Many sailors were taken prisoner when their ships were captured by the enemy. The British exchanged American soldiers they held, but they never freed captured sailors from prisons in England or prison ships. John Paul Jones knew conditions in these prisons were miserable. He was always concerned about these men and often wrote plans for getting them released.

His next step was to decide who to seize as a hostage so that prisoners could be freed. He really did not know the landed gentry. In fact, he knew only one lord, the Earl of Selkirk. His manor was on St. Mary's Isle, very near Arbigland, where Jones was born.

He sailed the *Ranger* toward St. Mary's Isle as soon as the Whitehaven raid was over. John Paul Jones intended to capture Lord Selkirk that very morning. He knew the waters were too shallow for the *Ranger,* so he and about a dozen men took off in the little ship's boat called a cutter. When they landed they told the workmen who met them that they were there to press men into the navy. Press meant to grab men and take them to work on ships; that is how navies got a lot of their men when there were not enough volunteers. With that news, of course, all the men on the estate ran and hid.

Lady Selkirk was so gracious to the raiders she even
gave them this silver teapot, with tea leaves
still in the bottom of it!

The *Ranger's* crew marched to the manor house, where they were
told that the Earl of Selkirk was not at home. John Paul Jones turned
around and started to walk back to the cutter. The first mate and the
marine lieutenant objected. If they could not seize a man, they
would loot the house. After all, the British had looted and burned
many homes in America. Captain Jones told them they could take
all the silver, or "plate," but they were not to take anything else. He
went to wait for them by the cutter.

When Lady Selkirk heard that her home was surrounded and
men were demanding the plate, she met them, and with great dig-
nity she said they were welcome to it. She even made sure they got
every piece there was, including the teapot full of tea leaves! The
sailors left and rowed back to the *Ranger.*

Lady Selkirk wrote to her husband telling him about the raid. She said that when she first met the men, she thought they were pirates and that Captain Jones was a great villain. John Paul Jones was a great admirer of women and he was very touched by Lady Selkirk's calm behavior. Perhaps he was a bit ashamed of what his crewmen had done for, about two weeks later, he wrote her a very long letter explaining why he led the raid and apologizing for it. He wrote that when the plate was sold, he would buy it back and return it to her.

The letter went on and on, even talking about the horrors of war and asking her to entreat her husband to get his government to end it. John Paul Jones was so taken with this letter that he sent her three copies. He also sent copies to Benjamin Franklin and the Marine Committee. Once again, he was writing to everyone to explain his actions.

But before he wrote that letter, and immediately after the raid, the captain decided on his next course of action. The *Ranger* would put out all sails and set out for the Irish coast and the North Channel. He and his men would continue to cruise in the Irish Sea.

5

The *Drake* and the *Bonhomme Richard*

In less than one day John Paul Jones had raided two places in England. Outraged citizens insisted that something be done about this pirate, so the British Admiralty sent two ships to the North Channel to catch him. Instead of sailing north and around Ireland to be safe, however, Captain Jones stayed right where he was.

He knew HMS *Drake* was in Belfast Lough. He had seen the sloop of war there before attacking Whitehaven. Now he meant to capture her by playing a trick. He stood the *Ranger* into the bay without flying his colors. Captain Burden of the *Drake* sent out a gig to see what ship this was. Captain Jones invited the lieutenant in the gig to come aboard, where he was promptly told he was a prisoner of Captain John Paul Jones of the American Navy. Captain Jones recorded in a letter that this tickled the crew who, under the rebellious Lieutenant Simpson, were getting ready to mutiny because they wanted more prize money. Their captain's trick inspired them to stay and do battle. They hoped to win prize money by capturing the *Drake*.

When they saw the gig being taken, the Irish people sensed there was going to be a good fight. They ran down to the shore to watch it. Some of them even rowed small boats out into the bay to be nearer the ships. John Paul Jones decided to fight in open water where he would have more room to maneuver. He headed out and let the *Drake* follow him until the ships were within hailing distance. The *Drake* raised her British ensign and the *Ranger* ran up the Stars and Stripes.

It was not long before the battle began. Captain Jones put the *Ranger* across the bow of and very close to the *Drake*. There was just about an hour of daylight left, so he wanted the fight to end quickly. He ordered his men to fire grapeshot at the British as fast as they could. The gunners were to aim for the men, the masts, and the sails. The ships were almost evenly matched; the *Drake* had two more guns than the *Ranger*. The Americans kept firing the grapeshot, being careful not to hit the hull. Their captain wanted the ship to stay afloat so he could tow her as a prize.

The battle lasted an hour and five minutes. First, Captain Burden was shot in the head. Then the *Drake's* second officer was badly wounded. The sails were torn and the rigging shot away. After that, there was not much the mate in charge of the *Drake* could do. He "called for quarter," which meant he surrendered.

The *Ranger's* crew was jubilant. They had another prize they could sell. John Paul Jones was happy too because he now had British sailors as prisoners, and he hoped to exchange them for American prisoners. He took the *Drake* in tow and sailed south. Soon the *Ranger* captured the brig *Patience*. Another prize to sell.

The British Admiralty sent more ships out to catch this American pirate. Let them try. John Paul Jones was not going to get caught. He turned to the north, planning to sail to France by going down the west coast of Ireland. Just to show his scorn for the Royal Navy, he put into Belfast Bay and released some fishermen he had captured. He gave them money and a new sail for their boat and they gave him three hurrahs.

Their flags flying, the *Ranger* and the *Drake*
are ready to begin fighting.

Lieutenant Simpson kept right on sailing to Brest, France,
rather than obeying the orders of John Paul Jones.

Captain Jones appointed Lieutenant Simpson commander of the
prize ship *Drake*. He was to stay near the *Ranger* and pay close attention to the signals that John Paul Jones would send. Off the coast
of France they spied a ship. The *Ranger* gave chase and hailed
Lieutenant Simpson to follow. Instead, the lieutenant kept right on
sailing to the port of Brest, France. Captain Jones was furious.
Lieutenant Simpson had been a troublemaker ever since they left
America. John Paul Jones would not have this insubordination. He
sent another lieutenant to take over the *Drake* and had Lieutenant
Simpson arrested. When they got to Brest on May 8, 1778, the captain refused to listen to the lieutenant, who argued he had not heard
the order and did not know he was to follow.

Most of the crew members sided with Lieutenant Simpson, but Captain Jones would not change his mind. He had the lieutenant put on a French prison ship. Simpson's supporters asked the American commissioners to help them free the lieutenant on parole. A short time later John Paul Jones agreed to release Lieutenant Simpson from his authority so that the lieutenant could become captain of the *Ranger* and sail her back to America with most of the crew. This was a hard and humiliating thing for John Paul Jones to do, but he wanted to stay in France to get command of a squadron.

Before the *Ranger* sailed, Lieutenant Simpson embarrassed Captain Jones further by boasting all over town about his appointment and saying that John Paul Jones was out of a job and not of much use to the navy. Again, the Scotsman's temper made him boiling mad. He felt the commissioners had shamed him by giving the *Ranger* to the lieutenant. The commissioners had many things to take care of and much on their minds. They were getting tired of hearing from John Paul Jones. Even Benjamin Franklin suggested to his friend that he go back to America, but the captain of the American Navy felt this was a disgraceful idea. He replied that he would rather die than go home before earning high honor and bringing glory to the navy.

What Captain Jones really wanted was to be made an admiral and given a fleet to command. He was determined to attack the British again. He went to Paris to try to get the *L'Indien,* the ship that had been promised to him once before, but the French had sold her. He then presented his ideas for naval raids to Monsieur de Sartine, the French Minister of Marine. If John Paul Jones could have a task force of two or three frigates, he could raid Scotland, Africa, and Newfoundland, capturing British privateers and warships all over the map. The French promised they would buy ships, but later they changed their mind. Captain Jones felt his honor was at stake. Instead of doing nothing on land, he should be on the seas attacking the enemy. He was, after all, America's best sailor.

He wrote letters to the three commissioners in France. He wrote to the statesman Robert Morris and Joseph Hewes in America. He

French statesman and soldier Marquis de Lafayette
was a friend of John Paul Jones.

even wrote to the King of France, Louis XVI! His letters annoyed a lot of the people he sent them to, but it is a good thing he wrote them. Many of them survived and today are in libraries and museums. By reading them we can get a good idea of John Paul Jones and the things he did during his adult life.

While he was fretting in France, the American Navy was having a hard time. In 1778 it lost nine frigates, and the British ruled the American seacoast. All the more reason for John Paul Jones to rule the British coast. His raids captured supplies the American Army needed and kept the Royal Navy busy hunting him. He kept looking everywhere for a ship to buy. He said that he wanted to get a ship that could sail fast because he intended "to go in harm's way."

Early in February 1779, nine long months after he fought the *Drake,* the French government bought the *Duc de Duras* and gave her to John Paul Jones to be refitted as a man-of-war. King Louis XVI said the gift of the ship was in honor of the daring captain's actions against the British. The French would pay to fit out the ship and would pay the crew as well.

Another Frenchman who admired Captain Jones was the Marquis de Lafayette. His affection for the captain, he exclaimed, would last forever. Lafayette had sailed back from America in April 1779 on the new frigate *Alliance.* He had been helping the Americans as a general in Washington's army. Now he wanted to help the navy. He made a plan whereby he and his soldiers would sail with John Paul Jones on the next raid and make a landing on the British coast. This was exactly what the captain wanted! He liked the idea so much that he had a roundhouse built on the deck of the new ship to house Lafayette and his staff.

The *Duc de Duras* was not really new; she was a thirteen-year-old merchant ship much heavier and larger than any ship John Paul Jones had commanded before. The first thing he did was change her name to the *Bonhomme Richard* to honor Benjamin Franklin. The French called Franklin's famous *Poor Richard's Almanack* "Les

The *Duc de Duras* was fitted out as a man-of-war and renamed
the *Bonhomme Richard* in honor of Benjamin Franklin.

Benjamin Franklin, as American envoy to Paris,
became a friend of the young sea captain.

Maximes du Bonhomme Richard." Then Captain Jones got busy
doing what he loved—fitting out the ship. In doing so he was following one of Poor Richard's sayings: "If you want something done
right, do it yourself."

He got new rigging and new spars for the ship. He had new ports
cut out for guns so that there would be two gun decks. Then he
went hunting for guns, which was not an easy task. He traveled all
over the part of France called Brittany and even went farther south

The cruises of the *Ranger* and the *Bonhomme Richard*.

to Angoulême. No wonder it took him more than six months to get the ship ready. Captain Jones eventually got sixteen new guns from the French Navy and twenty-four old ones from other ships.

The *Bonhomme Richard* was to fly the American flag even though it was a French ship. The French also said that John Paul Jones was to be in command of a squadron made up of various ships. The first was the *Alliance,* whose captain, Pierre Landais, had been in the French Navy since he was a young man. He had been made an honorary citizen of Massachusetts, but Landais was jealous of other captains, was not a reliable leader, and had a mutiny on his hands on the ship's first Atlantic crossing. Often in battle he acted as if he was against America. The other squadron ships were the brig *Vengeance,* the fast cutter *Cerf,* and the frigate *Pallas.* Their French commanding officers had been given commissions in the American Navy.

Monsieur de Sartine gave John Paul Jones these orders: he could sail whenever he was ready, go anywhere he decided to, and set his own course of action. After months of waiting and hard work, John Paul Jones set sail to cruise in harm's way and find glory.

6

The Battle of Flamborough Head

Captain Jones was pleased with his crew, which came to a grand total of 360 officers, seamen, and volunteers. He had visited all the nearby docks to find good sailors for his squadron, and he had chosen the officers carefully. They all worked well together.

First Lieutenant Richard Dale was from Virginia. John Paul Jones trusted him so much he called him "good old Dick." Lieutenant Dale had escaped from an English prison and volunteered for the *Bonhomme Richard*. He was eager to fight the British. Second Lieutenant Henry Lunt had been with Captain Jones in the *Providence* and knew the captain's way of cruising. He too had been in an English prison, and the captain was very happy to see him free and have him on board. Midshipman Nathaniel Fanning, a brave sailor from New England, had been in prison and was freed when prisoners were exchanged.

The seamen were volunteers who liked fighting. There was a mix of Americans, French, Portuguese, Dutch, and Danish sailors. Some English prisoners had also volunteered to join the crew, but they

This banner honors American naval heroes, including
John Paul Jones and Richard Dale.

plotted mutiny and rebelled. John Paul Jones gave their ringleader 250 lashes on his back and sent him ashore to prison. He fired the rest of them.

On June 19, 1779, the squadron sailed from the seaport Lorient, escorting some merchant ships to Bordeaux. They had hardly gotten under way when the *Bonhomme Richard* and *Alliance* fouled each other, breaking masts and spars. John Paul Jones believed that Captain Landais had caused the accident by not paying attention to his signals. Nevertheless, the blame was put on the *Bonhomme Richard*'s officer of the deck, Lieutenant Robinson, who was court-martialed and dismissed. This left Captain Landais free to insult Captain Jones, to complain about his orders, or to ignore them because he wanted to be the one in command.

During July, while the ships were being repaired, John Paul Jones prepared for a long cruise. The French changed his orders. He was to sail to the north of Britain and destroy merchant ships along the way. After six weeks he was to take the squadron to the Texel in the Netherlands and await further orders. These orders suited Captain Jones just fine. He could still do as he pleased. His squadron was to pay close attention to the signals hoisted on the *Bonhomme Richard*. No ship was to chase another ship by itself. Each captain was given a list of places to meet the other ships if he got separated.

On August fourteenth the flagship *Bonhomme Richard*, the frigates *Alliance* and *Pallas*, the brig *Vengeance*, the cutter *Cerf*, and two privateers, the *Monsieur* and *Granville*, sailed out with ensigns flying. They started up the west coast of Ireland and soon captured two brigs, which they sent back to France with prize crews on board. Then the two merchant ships left the squadron because they wanted to sail somewhere else. The cutter left later on because of high seas.

John Paul Jones, however, kept right on sailing and capturing prizes. Off the Outer Hebrides his crew caught the *Union*, full of clothing for the British army in Canada. Then they captured two colliers from Leith. As they were sailing down the east coast of

Another of the ports on the Bay of Biscay, Lorient as it looked
at the time of the American Revolution.

Scotland, Captain Jones decided to land there and hold its officials
for ransom, believing they could be traded for prisoners.

By now everybody along the coast was alarmed. The "pirate" was
back. The Admiralty had sent ships out to find him, but they had
gone up the wrong coast of Ireland. The people along the shore were
packing their goods and preparing to leave their houses, and coastal
vessels were going into safe harbors. In Leith and nearby Edinburgh,
the drums were beating and the citizens were fleeing. The *Bonhomme Richard* almost got within cannon shot of Leith, but luckily
for the Scots, a gale came up suddenly and John Paul Jones had to
put back to sea. He started down the North Sea coast again.

While all this was going on, Captain Richard Pearson of HMS
Serapis was convoying a large group of merchant ships across the
North Sea from Denmark. He and the sloop *Countess of Scarborough*

This portrait by Arthur Conrad shows Captain Jones
in his tricornered hat and handsome uniform.

had seventy ships to protect. The *Serapis* was a new ship with a new innovation—a copper bottom that helped her sail fast. She had fifty guns and a well-disciplined crew of three hundred who thought that one good British tar was worth three Yankee sailors.

Sailing along with a telescope to his eye, Captain Pearson began to notice red flags flying along the coast. These were the signal for

Captain Richard Pearson of HMS *Serapis.*

danger. As he spotted the red flag flying from the castle in Scarborough, a cutter came out to the *Serapis* with a letter for the captain. The letter said John Paul Jones the pirate was back again and had been spied standing south for Flamborough Head, just south of there. Captain Pearson ran up signal flags telling the convoy to sail north, then fired guns to bring attention to his command. They were all to keep close to shore.

As the *Serapis* came abreast of Flamborough Head at one o'clock on September twenty-third, Captain Pearson spotted four ships flying British colors. He knew it was the enemy's squadron. The *Bonhomme Richard's* lookout yelled "sail ho," and John Paul Jones brought the ships quickly around to stand north, toward this large ship. He stood on the deck looking every inch the man in command, wearing a blue-and-white coat decorated with gold buttons and two epaulets, white breeches, and a tricornered hat. He loved to wear a smart uniform and was always neatly dressed.

Captain Jones called for battle stations; so did Captain Pearson. Then the former signaled for the squadron to form a line of battle. This was what Captain Pearson thought would happen—that all the enemy ships would shoot at him at once. Imagine his surprise when the *Alliance* headed off for open water. Then the *Pallas* sailed off, and the *Vengeance* did not get in line. John Paul Jones was left to fight alone.

Captain Jones ran up the signal for general chase. On both ships things began to happen very fast. Drummers beat a rapid tattoo telling the gun crews to get ready. All three mainsails were hauled up because if they were unfurled, they would block the view and could be set afire. The decks were sloshed down with water so that spilled gunpowder would not catch fire. Huge casks of water were close at hand with which to sponge the cannons. In the cockpit the ships' surgeons were preparing canvas to put wounded sailors on, tubs of water to wash the wounds, bandages, and spirits to deaden the pain when arm or leg had to be sawed off.

Each mast on a ship had a platform near the top. The one on the foremast of the *Bonhomme Richard* was forty feet above the deck. Captain Jones sent fourteen sharpshooters under Midshipman Fanning's direction scrambling up to this fighting top. They were armed with swivel guns, muskets, coehorns, and grenades. Captain Jones sent twenty others to the mainmast platform and nine to the mizzenmast lookout. They were to shoot enemy sailors as quickly as they could.

Successive Positions in the Battle off Flamborough Head.

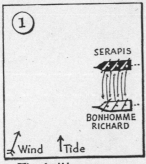

① The battle opens.

SERAPIS
BONHOMME RICHARD

Wind Tide

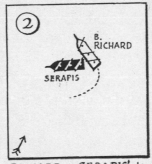

② RICHARD on SERAPIS' starboard quarter, hoping to board.

B. RICHARD
SERAPIS

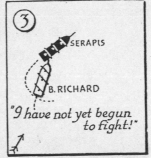

③ SERAPIS tries to cross RICHARD'S bow, but has not enough headway. RICHARD'S bowsprit hits SERAPIS.

SERAPIS
B. RICHARD

"I have not yet begun to fight!"

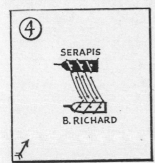

④ They straighten out again. SERAPIS backs topsails to reduce speed.

SERAPIS
B. RICHARD

⑤ RICHARD surges ahead, tries to cross SERAPIS' bow, her jib boom fouls RICHARD'S mizzen shrouds.

B. RICHARD
SERAPIS

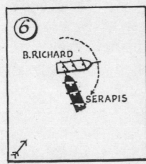

⑥ RICHARD pivots on SERAPIS' bowsprit.

B. RICHARD
SERAPIS

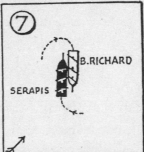

⑦ They fall alongside, grappled. Night falls.

B. RICHARD
SERAPIS

⑧ 3rd broadside
B. RICHARD
SERAPIS
ALLIANCE
2nd broadside
Tide

SERAPIS, anchored and locked to RICHARD, swings 180° with tide. They fight for two hours, when SERAPIS strikes. ALLIANCE sails around them firing broadsides mostly at RICHARD.

These drawings show the stages in the battle between the *Serapis* and the *Bonhomme Richard* at Flamborough Head.

It was now seven o'clock at night. A slight wind was blowing and a harvest moon was rising. The British captain hailed the *Bonhomme Richard,* and John Paul Jones replied that his ship was the *Princess Royal.* Captain Pearson hailed the ship a second time. The third time he hailed, Captain Jones broke out the Stars and Stripes and began firing.

The *Serapis* fired right back and tore some holes in the *Bonhomme Richard* at the water line. The ship's carpenter rushed up with shot plugs (wooden pegs covered with oakum) to try to repair the leaks. Then, when some of the *Bonhomme Richard's* old guns were fired, they exploded, killing or wounding their gun crews and setting fires on the deck. The *Serapis's* gunnery was accurate; the third time her crew fired, the shot sliced the American ship's sails, cut the rigging, tore holes in the planking, and killed a number of the French marines on board. Now John Paul Jones had just twelve guns left in his main battery.

Captain Jones decided the only way he could win was to grapple and board the enemy ship. But first he had to get rid of the British sharpshooters on their platforms by shooting and hurling grenades at them. He crashed his bow into the *Serapis's* port side and tried to attach grapple hooks, but they were cut apart by axes and the ships hauled off. Then they were bow to bow, side by side, again, and the *Serapis* fired as fast as possible. The night was getting darker, cannons were flashing, fires were burning with bright flames, and smoke was billowing everywhere. John Paul Jones recalled later that it was a fury that never ended.

By this time more than one thousand spectators had come in carriages or on horseback to Flamborough Head. They had heard that the pirate had been cornered, and they came to watch him get caught.

A slight breeze came up and helped Captain Jones swing across Captain Pearson's bow. The *Serapis's* bowsprit hit the *Bonhomme Richard,* locking the two ships together, side by side. The British guns kept pounding, and Captain Pearson asked Captain Jones if he

The battle continued on into the night.

One artist's way of depicting what John Paul Jones called
"the fury that never ended."

was ready to surrender. After all, the *Bonhomme Richard* was riddled with so many holes, you could see in one side and out the other!

John Paul Jones shouted back his famous answer: "I have not yet begun to fight."

Then he took the place of a wounded gunnery officer and helped drag a three-thousand-pound gun from the other side of the ship. John Paul Jones aimed at the enemy's mainmast knowing that if it came down, Captain Pearson would have to surrender. Just then the *Alliance* came into view, and John Paul Jones thought he was getting much needed help at last. To his utter amazement, the *Alliance*

Pierre Landais fired on the *Bonhomme Richard*
instead of coming to her aid!

sailed around the two warships and fired into the *Bonhomme Richard,* killing her men. To have a ship of his own squadron hit him with cannonballs was almost too much for the captain. He was so tired, he sat down on the deck. A young sailor came up to him and asked why he did not strike, which meant to lower the flag and surrender. "I will never surrender. I will sink first," John Paul Jones told him, and he jumped up to help with the guns.

At this point, William Hamilton, a volunteer, did a very brave thing. He crawled out onto the main yardarm carrying a bucket full of grenades. He held a smoldering slow match to light them

By the end of the battle, all the sails were
shot full of holes.

with in his teeth. When he got to the platform, Hamilton began to hurl grenades onto the *Serapis's* deck. As luck would have it, one went through an open hatch. It blew up on the lower gun deck, setting gunpowder on fire, smashing guns, and causing a dreadful explosion.

By then fires were ablaze all over the *Bonhomme Richard.* Her whole side had been shot away, and there were so many holes in the hull, seven feet of water had risen in the hold. Again the *Alliance* came up, but again, when he was only fifty yards away, Captain Landais fired at both ships. The hold was full of prisoners taken from the prize ships, and they were afraid of drowning. They began to panic. Some petty officers set them free, and they scrambled up on deck to try to leap over to the *Serapis.* But Lieutenant Dale got them back under control and put them to work pumping out the water.

The battle had gone on for more than three hours, and it looked as if the *Bonhomme Richard* could not stay afloat. Many of her officers urged John Paul Jones to surrender. Just then the *Serapis's* mainmast came crashing down. Captain Pearson yelled to John Paul Jones that he was striking his colors. He hauled down the British ensign. Lieutenant Dale boarded the *Serapis* to escort the defeated captain to the *Bonhomme Richard.* Captain Pearson handed over his sword to Captain Jones, but John Paul Jones gave it back and invited him to what was left of his quarters for a friendly glass of wine.

7

Fame and Glory

For three and a half hours John Paul Jones had fought and refused to surrender a sinking ship. Now the sight that greeted him was almost too terrible to look at. The decks of his ship were awash with blood and full of dead and wounded men. Fires were burning everywhere, and water was pouring in through the holes made by the enemy's cannons. For almost two days after the battle the crew worked as hard as they could to save the brave ship. They put out fires, tried to plug holes, and manned the pumps. The ship's surgeon and crew members did their best to aid the wounded. They buried the dead with honors at sea. Finally, the captain knew he could not save his ship, and he transferred his flag to the *Serapis*. He sent Captain Pearson to stay on the *Pallas*.

Lieutenant Dale cut the *Serapis's* anchor cable and the ship slowly got under way, sailing east. She stood by the *Bonhomme Richard*, trying to ease her across the North Sea to port. But the gallant ship could not make it. With sails set and pennants flying, she went to a watery grave. The other ships of the squadron continued

Only the top of the *Bonhomme Richard*'s mainmast shows
as the last of her crew row to the *Serapis*.

Captain Jones and his men standing on the deck of the *Serapis*
as they bid farewell to the battered *Bonhomme Richard*
going to her watery grave.

on to the Texel, the safe harbor of Amsterdam where Captain Jones had been ordered to go. They arrived on October 3, 1779, and stayed there almost the rest of the year.

When news of the great battle reached England, there was more of an uproar than when John Paul Jones had raided Whitehaven and taken the *Drake*. The British drew cartoons of him dressed as a pirate with six guns at his waist. They made up stories about his cruel actions. In Paris and Versailles, however, they talked of his cool conduct and bravery. The French said his actions would make him famous forever.

The Dutch people hailed him too, making up a song that began, "Here comes Paul Jones, such a nice man." What the nice man was trying to do was get all the wounded on shore and arrange an exchange of more than five hundred prisoners. He had always worked hard to free prisoners. Three of his best volunteers during the Battle at Flamborough Head had been former prisoners in England.

The British wanted to take the American Navy captain prisoner, but they could not get the Dutch to hand him over. So they put a squadron at the entrance to the Texel. They intended to trap John Paul Jones when he was leaving.

When he did sail out of the Texel, it was as captain of the *Alliance*. The French government had taken back their ships, as well as the captured *Serapis,* and they sent Captain Landais to Paris to give reason for his cowardly actions. Captain Landais left the *Alliance* a filthy mess, low on supplies, and with an idle crew. Captain Jones had her careened, cleaned, and new supplies of hardtack, salt beef, coffee, sugar, and liquor stored on board.

On December twenty-seventh, while an east wind temporarily blew the British blockaders away, John Paul Jones raised the Stars and Stripes and sailed out of the Texel, keeping close to the shoreline. He was at sea again, which he loved. He could not resist cruising, in case he could capture more ships. He did overcome one small English brig. Later the *Alliance* stopped in Spain for more

John Paul Jones sailed the *Alliance* out of the Texel
without being captured by the British.

food, wood, and water. The captain and crew did not get back to Lorient until February 10, 1780.

The American colonies still needed supplies for their fight against the British. Benjamin Franklin urged John Paul Jones to sail home with a huge supply of muskets, which Lafayette had gotten, and bales of cloth for uniforms. But instead of sailing, he was off to Paris because his crew were demanding pay and prize money.

It is sad to tell, but a good deal of his time in the navy was not spent on board a ship. Instead, John Paul Jones was on land trying to sell prize ships to get the money due him and his crew. Part of the problem was that America did not have any money. One of the main reasons Benjamin Franklin was in Paris was to try to get other countries to lend the colonists money. The prize ships he captured had

The ladies in France greeted the conquering naval
hero warmly, and he loved their attention.

been taken to Denmark, Holland, and France. Thus, he had to deal
with the laws of three different countries. It took time and hard work,
but this also gave him a chance to meet high officials and pretty ladies.

When John Paul Jones got to Paris in April he was overcome
with the honors that were heaped on him. He was wined and dined
and flattered by the ladies. One of them called him "adorable Jones."
He admitted he did love the ladies. He never married, but he often

John Paul Jones liked this bust of himself by French sculptor Jean-Antoine Houdon so much that he had copies made of it to give to his friends.

talked and wrote about his affairs of the heart. When he was out in society he was soft spoken and mild mannered. No wonder the ladies flocked to this courteous naval hero in his fancy uniform. He never lost his temper when he was with them.

The Freemasons honored him with a tribute from the Lodge of the Nine Sisters. His highest honor came from King Louis XVI. It was a sword with a gold hilt that was inscribed to the man who defended the "Freedom of the Seas." The king also proposed that he be named to the Order of Military Merit. John Paul Jones had to get permission from the Continental Congress to accept this medal. He then had the right to the title "Chevalier," which he sometimes used in signing his letters. No other naval officer in America was able to do this.

The noted French sculptor Jean-Antoine Houdon made a marble bust of John Paul Jones which is considered the best likeness of him ever made. The vain captain was so puffed up by this that he had many copies of the bust made to give to his friends.

The hero enjoyed the social life in Paris so much that he stayed and stayed. He did not leave France until October, when he was to sail as captain of the sloop *Ariel*. Before he left, John Paul Jones held a grand party. At least that is what Midshipman Fanning wrote in his book about his famous captain. He reported that a room with canvas walls was made on the quarterdeck of the *Ariel*. The walls were lined with pink silk and hung with pictures and mirrors. A banquet that lasted for hours was accompanied by toasts and thirteen-gun salutes, a band, and fireworks. Captain Jones entertained his lady friends in grand style.

As the *Ariel* sailed west on October ninth, she ran into a fierce storm off Penmarch Rocks, a dangerous spot for any vessel. Once again John Paul Jones proved his naval genius. He paid out the anchors and then cut away the foremast and mainmast, which took the mizzenmast with it as it fell. But the anchors held and the *Ariel* rode out the storm. Then the crew rigged new masts by tying

John Paul Jones loved to fit out a new ship. Here, he is depicted watching the *America* being built in Portsmouth, New Hampshire.

broken pieces together, and they sailed back to France for repairs. Finally, in December, they left for America.

The *Ariel* reached Philadelphia early in 1781, and John Paul Jones stayed there for six months trying to get the back pay due him. Congress began an investigation of his conduct and that of the *Alliance* during the battle with the *Serapis*. They asked him forty-seven questions, and he answered them so well in writing that Congress held him in high esteem and voted him a formal resolution of thanks. They also selected him to be commanding officer of the new ship *America* and sent him to Portsmouth to fit her out.

In October 1781 General Charles Cornwallis surrendered to George Washington at Yorktown and the American Revolution ended. The new country felt there was no need for a navy at all, and they gave the *America* to France.

8

The Captain's Last Days

Captain John Paul Jones, America's most famous naval officer, was without a ship to command. Often in his letters he had written that the country would always need a strong navy. But America was a young country, and Congress had other things to think about. It had to write a constitution so that there would be laws. It had to elect its first president and find a city for the capitol. It had to find a way to make money to run the government. It did not have time to think of ships, so the few that remained at the end of the war were sold and their crews disbanded.

On November 10, 1783, John Paul Jones left America to go back to Paris to live. He knew many of the aristocrats and had a cordial time in their society. Once again he spent time trying to get the money for the prizes he had captured. He wrote a journal of his life from 1775–1784, had it bound in red leather, and gave it to King Louis XVI. He went back to America for a visit in 1787 to try to get himself promoted to rear admiral. He really wanted to be named

The Continental Congress awarded Captain Jones
this gold medal.

admiral of the fleet. Instead, Congress presented him with a gold medal inscribed to the commander of the fleet.

When John Paul Jones got back to Paris later that year he met Thomas Jefferson, who was there as America's ambassador. Thomas Jefferson told him that Catherine the Great, Empress of Russia, wanted John Paul Jones to head a fleet to attack and defeat the Turks in the Black Sea. At last he would get the opportunity to go to sea again and be in command of a squadron. John Paul Jones jumped at

Titled *Commodore John Paul Jones: American Revolution 1747–1792*, this portrait was painted by Cecilia Beaux.

the chance, and after a cold, windy trip across the ice-laden Baltic Sea, he landed at St. Petersburg on May 2, 1788. Imagine his delight when he was named Kontradmiral Pavel Ivanovich Jones—Rear Admiral John Paul Jones.

For two weeks the Russians entertained him and treated him to all sorts of flattery. He was given the flagship *Vladimir,* but his command was held jointly with Field Marshal Prince Potemkin, a great favorite of Catherine the Great. Of course, a joint command of two hot-tempered, egotistic men would never work. The Russian naval officers who served under John Paul Jones had nothing but praise for him, but Prince Potemkin made fun of him all the time and often changed his orders. He reported to the empress that Rear Admiral Jones was not a success, and she recalled him to St. Petersburg. Catherine the Great gave him two years' advance pay and dismissed him from her service. The rear admiral was once again simply Commander John Paul Jones.

He went back to Paris in May 1790. He was a saddened man and his health was poor. In his letters he spoke of "very bad health." He kept writing to Catherine the Great, explaining his actions with the Russian Fleet. He was certain that if his plans had been followed, the Russian Navy would have defeated the Turks.

Ever since he left home as a young boy, John Paul Jones had kept in touch with his family. Now he wrote to his sisters about patching up a quarrel two of them had had with each other. Sometimes he did favors for other people. For example, he wrote some German merchants and ordered smoked beef to be sent to his friend Thomas Jefferson. John Paul Jones had gotten beautiful furs in Russia for King Louis XVI and Lafayette, and he wrote to Lafayette about them.

Life in Paris was not the gay round of parties it used to be. The French people were getting ready to overthrow King Louis XVI, and most of the American Navy hero's friends had fled. Only a few were left. He spent time lying in the hammock in the back yard of his apartment. His hair was gray, he coughed a lot, and his legs were swollen.

On July 18, 1792, John Paul Jones stumbled to his bed, stretched out across it, and died—alone. He was forty-five years old.

His friends wrapped his body in a winding-sheet and placed it in a lead coffin. He was buried in a little cemetery outside the walls of Paris that had been set aside for foreigners who were Protestants. Only two Americans walked in the procession to his grave. Free-masons from the Lodge of the Nine Sisters honored him by attend-ing the service. The French officials who loved John Paul Jones sent a detachment of grenadiers to lead the hearse. Monsieur Paul-Henri Marron, who led the funeral service, predicted that his noble patrio-tism would be revered by future generations.

But the naval hero of the American Revolution was soon forgot-ten by the new country for which he had fought. It was not until 1796 that Congress voted to establish a permanent navy. The Con-gress in 1834 voted to name a ship for John Paul Jones, but the ship was not built until years later. Then, in 1845, Secretary of the Navy George Bancroft, who founded the United States Naval Academy, tried to get the coffin of John Paul Jones brought to America. The government was not interested in doing this.

In 1898, General Horace Porter was named the United States ambassador to France. By that time the United States had a very good navy. It had just helped win the Spanish-American War by defeating Spanish ships at Santiago, Chile. Admiral George Dewey's fleet had captured Manila in the Philippines. Ambassador Porter began to think of America's sailor—the man who had insisted on a strong navy—and decided to find his grave. It took him almost five years. He had to look in many official documents, church ledgers, and old newspapers. Finally, he learned that the grave was in St. Louis Cemetery, but the cemetery could not be seen. As Paris grew, buildings had spread out and covered the land, including all the graves. That meant that they were under buildings, deep in the ground.

The U.S. Navy finally did name a ship—this guided missile destroyer—in honor of John Paul Jones.

It also meant the ambassador had to get permission to dig under the buildings. His crew dug five shafts down into the ground and then tunnels going off from these shafts. They found only five lead coffins; the rest were wooden and had crumbled away. Three of the lead coffins had nameplates on them. One of the other two was long enough for a person over six feet tall. Porter and his crew decided the remaining one had to be the one holding the remains of John Paul Jones. When they opened the coffin they found that the body had been well preserved with alcohol and was carefully packed with straw. This was because John Paul Jones's friends had packed his body so it would travel safely across the ocean.

Staff of the Ecole de Médicine were called in, and after studying the body, they announced that these were indeed the remains of

The search for the navy captain's grave took the diggers
beneath buildings in Paris.

The lead coffin was finally found that contained the remains of John Paul Jones.

John Paul Jones. They noted that his hair was in a little cap that had the letter "J" on it and that one of the earlobes exactly matched the earlobe on Houdon's bust of the captain.

At that time Theodore Roosevelt was president of the United States. He had always been in favor of a strong navy and was delighted that the body of America's sailor had been found. Everyone—Ambassador Porter, President Roosevelt, and the French government—decided to send the coffin to America with all the honor John Paul Jones deserved. President Roosevelt sent four cruisers to France to bring the body back. The flagship, the USS *Brooklyn,* was under the command of Rear Admiral Charles D. Sigsbee. Captain Jones would have loved this squadron; it was exactly the kind he had wanted to command.

The coffin of John Paul Jones was transported to the USS *Brooklyn* for the trip to Annapolis, Maryland.

On July 6, 1905, 158 years after John Paul Jones was born, a special service was held for him in the American Church in Paris. Then his coffin, which had since been encased in a mahogany one, was carried to the train station on a horse-drawn wagon. Five hundred people—American sailors, high government officials, and French cavalry and soldiers—paraded with the coffin. A special train carried it to Cherbourg where it was piped aboard the *Brooklyn*. When the squadron got to America it was joined by seven other ships. Then all eleven ships steamed to Annapolis, Maryland, home of the United States Naval Academy. An elaborate ceremony was held to commemorate the event, during which President Roosevelt gave a fine speech.

On April 24, 1906, an elaborate ceremony was held at the
U.S. Naval Academy in Annapolis, Maryland, to welcome
John Paul Jones "home."

Congress voted funds to build a resting place for the man who knew the importance of a navy. On January 26, 1913, John Paul Jones, America's sailor, was laid to final rest in a green marble sarcophagus in the crypt of the Naval Academy's chapel.

A guard of honor stands watch at the crypt every day. That is America's way of honoring the sailor who taught that:

★ A naval officer should be well educated

★ A naval officer should have very good manners

★ A naval officer should know the laws of the seas and of other countries

★ A naval officer should reward or punish subordinates fairly

★ A naval officer should be the absolute ruler of the ship.

The sarcophagus for John Paul Jones rests in the crypt of the Naval Academy Chapel.

Charles Henry Niehaus's statue of America's sailor
stands near the Tidal Basin in Washington, D.C.

When Some Things Happened

1747   John Paul born on July 6 in Scotland

1761   John Paul apprenticed to James Younger

1768   John Paul sailed on the brig *John*

1770   Carpenter Mungo Maxwell lashed for disobeying orders;
warrant out in England for John Paul's arrest;
John Paul joins St. Bernard's Masonic Lodge in
Kirkcudbright

1772   John Paul bought the merchant ship *Betsy*

1773   John Paul accidentally killed a sailor during an uprising;
he fled Tobago and went into hiding; Boston Tea Party

1774   First Continental Congress met in Philadelphia

1775   Battle of Lexington and Concord, April 18; Naval Committee picked Esek Hopkins to head fleet; John Paul Jones commissioned first lieutenant, December 7

1776   John Paul Jones sailed in the *Alfred* with fleet to the Bahamas; given command of the *Providence*; cruised in Atlantic; commissioned captain, August 8

1777   John Paul Jones given command of the *Ranger* on June 14; Stars and Stripes become national flag on June 14; General Burgoyne surrendered army at Saratoga in October; John Paul Jones sailed the *Ranger* to France on November 1

1778   John Paul Jones raided Whitehaven harbor on April 22; crew stole silver plate from Lady Selkirk; John Paul Jones had Lieutenant Simpson arrested for disobeying orders; the *Ranger* reached port of Brest on May 8

1779   French gave John Paul Jones the *Duc de Duras* in February; ship renamed *Bonhomme Richard*; he and his crew cruised up the west side of Ireland in August; they engaged the British in the Battle of Flamborough Head on September 23; arrived at the Texel on October 3; escaped on December 27

1780   John Paul Jones returned to Lorient, France

1781   John Paul Jones arrived in Philadelphia in the *Ariel*; Lord Cornwallis surrendered in October

1788   John Paul Jones arrived in St. Petersburg to serve Catherine the Great

1790   John Paul Jones returned to Paris

1792   John Paul Jones died in Paris on July 18

1905   John Paul Jones's coffin brought to the United
        States Naval Academy

1913   John Paul Jones was laid to final rest in the Naval
        Academy Chapel on January 26

Glossary

Boatswain	Officer in charge of a ship's deck crew
Bow	Front end of a ship
Breeches	Pants that come just below the knee
Brig	Two-masted, square-rigged sailing ship (like the *Friendship* or *Vengeance*)
Careen	To lean a ship on its side
Coehorn	Small mortar for throwing grenades
Collier	Coal boat
Cutter	Ship's boat for carrying cargo or passengers
Foul	To entangle

Frigate	Fast-sailing warship, usually three masted and square-rigged (like the *Ranger*, *L'Indien*, or *Alliance*)
Galley	Ship's kitchen
Gig	Fast, light rowboat
Grapeshot	Cluster of small iron balls
Grapple	To attach with a hook
Greaved	To put a boat up on a sandy beach
Hessian	Burlap
Hold	Interior of a ship, below deck
Hove	To come to position
Hull	Main body of a ship
Lough	Bay or inlet (pronounced *lock*)
Oakum	Fiber used for caulking
Plate	Silver tea service
Powder horn	Container for gunpowder
Quoin	Wedge-shaped piece of wood
Roundhouse	Cabin on the stern of a ship's quarterdeck

Schooner Ship with a mast fore and aft, plus a foremast and a mainmast amidships (like the *Hannah*)

Scuttlebutt Cask to hold drinking water

Sloop One-masted ship with a long bowsprit (like the *Providence* and *Ariel*)

Spar Stout wood piece (as a mast or boom) to support rigging

Spike To pierce with a sharp piece of metal

Stern Back end of a ship

Swivel Small gun on a support that turns

Tar Sailor

Tattoo Any signal that is beat on a drum

Tompion Stopper, or plug, for the muzzle of a cannon

Tricorn Hat with a brim turned up on three sides

Yardarm End of a wooden pole that supports a sail

Some Books Used to Write This Story

Allen, Gardner W. *A Naval History of the American Revolution.* Williamstown: Corner House Publishing, 1970.

Barnes, John S., edited and annotated by. *Fanning's Narrative, Being the Memoirs of Nathaniel Fanning Officer of the Revolutionary War 1778–1783.* New York: n.p., 1812.

Brown, Charles Walter. *John Paul Jones of Naval Fame, A Character of the Revolution.* Chicago: M. A. Donahue Co., 1902.

Chapelle, Howard I. *The History of the American Sailing Navy.* New York: W. W. Norton & Co., 1935.

Herbert, Charles. *A Relic of the Revolution.* Boston: n.p., 1847.

Lorenz, Lincoln. *The Admiral and the Empress, John Paul Jones and Catherine the Great.* New York: Bookman Assoc., 1954.

Morison, Samuel Eliot. *John Paul Jones, A Sailor's Biography.* Boston: Little, Brown & Co., 1959.

Walsh, John Evangelist. *Night on Fire.* New York: McGraw-Hill Book Company, 1978.

Index

A number in italic type indicates an illustration on that page.

Index

Picture Credits

The pictures in this book are used with the kind permission of the following:

Author: 8, 9
The Beverley R. Robinson Collection, U.S. Naval Academy
  Museum: 14, 35, 41, 51, 59, 61, 62, 69
The Dumfries & Galloway Council: 5
The Mariners' Museum, Newport News, Virginia: 6
The Peabody Essex Museum, Salem, Massachusetts: 29
The Samuel Loring Morison Collection: 15, 37, 42, 53, 55, 57
Special Collections and Archives Division, Nimitz Library, U.S.
  Naval Academy: 2, 22, 32, 79, 80
The U.S. Naval Academy Archives: 83
The U.S. Naval Institute Photographic Library: frontispiece, 18, 21,
  25, 27, 44, 46, 47, 48 (courtesy of Craig L. Symonds), 54, 60,
  66, 68, 70, 74 (courtesy of the U.S. Naval Academy Museum),
  75, 78, 81, 82, 84
William Gilkerson, The Beverley R. Robinson Collection, U.S.
  Naval Academy Museum: 20, 33, 65, 72

Note: The drawings of the slave ship on page 11 came from Clarkson's *Abolition of the Slave Trade,* London, 1808.

About the Author

Clara Ann Simmons was born and grew up in Johnstown, Pennsylvania. Now she lives on the Eastern Shore of Maryland. When she isn't researching and writing, she likes to spend her time reading, traveling, and being with her family. Her book *The Story of the U.S. Naval Academy* was published by the Naval Institute Press in 1995.

The Naval Institute Press is the book-publishing arm of the U.S. Naval Institute, a private, nonprofit, membership society for sea service professionals and others who share an interest in naval and maritime affairs. Established in 1873 at the U.S. Naval Academy in Annapolis, Maryland, where its offices remain today, the Naval Institute has members worldwide.

Members of the Naval Institute support the education programs of the society and receive the influential monthly magazine *Proceedings* and discounts on fine nautical prints and on ship and aircraft photos. They also have access to the transcripts of the Institute's Oral History Program and get discounted admission to any of the Institute-sponsored seminars offered around the country.

The Naval Institute also publishes *Naval History* magazine. This colorful bimonthly is filled with entertaining and thought-provoking articles, first-person reminiscences, and dramatic art and photography. Members receive a discount on *Naval History* subscriptions.

The Naval Institute's book-publishing program, begun in 1898 with basic guides to naval practices, has broadened its scope in recent years to include books of more general interest. Now the Naval Institute Press publishes about 100 titles each year, ranging from how-to books on boating and navigation to battle histories, biographies, ship and aircraft guides, and novels. Institute members receive discounts of 20 to 50 percent on the Press's nearly 600 books in print.

Full-time students are eligible for special half-price membership rates. Life memberships are also available.

For a free catalog describing Naval Institute Press books currently available, and for further information about subscribing to *Naval History* magazine or about joining the U.S. Naval Institute, please write to:

Membership Department
U.S. Naval Institute
118 Maryland Avenue
Annapolis, MD 21402-5035
Telephone: (800) 233-8764
Fax: (410) 269-7940
Web address: www.usni.org